$11.95

3-90

Recent Books

D1540766

The
Black
Death

by
Timothy Levi Biel

Illustrations by
Maurie Manning and Michael Spackman

LUCENT
B·O·O·K·S

WORLD DISASTERS

Look for these and other exciting World Disaster books:

Pompeii
The Titanic
The San Francisco Earthquake
The Chicago Fire
The Dust Bowl
The Crash of '29
The Armenian Earthquake

Library of Congress Cataloging-in-Publication Data

Biel, Timothy L., 1950-
    The black death / by Timothy Levi Biel ; illustrations by Maurie Manning and Michael Spackman.
        p.   cm. -- (World disasters)
    Bibliography: p.
    Includes index.
    Summary: Describes the social and economic conditions in medieval Europe at the outbreak of the Black Death and the causes and effects of the epidemic.
    ISBN 1-56006-001-8 :
    1. Black death--Europe--History--Juvenile literature.   [1. Black Death. 2. Plague.] I. Manning, Maurie 1960- ill. II. Title III. Series.
    RC178.A1B54 1989
    614.4'94--dc20   89-112269
                                                                                            CIP
                                                                                            AC

To my parents, Kenneth & Caroline Biel

Table of Contents

Preface
The World Disasters Series

World disasters have always aroused human curiosity. Whenever news of tragedy spreads, we want to learn more about it. We wonder how and why the disaster happened, how people reacted, and whether we might have acted differently. To be sure, disaster evokes a wide range of responses—fear, sorrow, despair, generosity, even hope. Yet from every great disaster, one remarkable truth always seems to emerge: in spite of death, pain, and destruction, the human spirit triumphs.

History is full of great disasters, which arise from a variety of causes. Earthquakes, floods, volcanic eruptions, and other natural events often produce widespread destruction. Just as often, however, people accidentally bring suffering and distress on themselves and other human beings. And many disasters have sinister causes, like human greed, envy, or prejudice.

The disasters included in this series have been chosen not only for their dramatic qualities, but also for their educational value. The reader will learn about the causes and effects of the greatest disasters in history. Technical concepts and interesting anecdotes are explained and illustrated in inset boxes.

But disasters should not be viewed in isolation. To enrich the reader's understanding, these books present historical information about the time period, and interesting facts about the culture in which each disaster occurred. Finally, they teach valuable lessons about human nature. More acts of bravery, cowardice, intelligence, and foolishness are compressed into the few days of a disaster than most people experience in a lifetime.

Dramatic illustrations and evocative narrative lure the reader to distant cities and times gone by. Readers witness the awesome power of an exploding volcano, the magnitude of a violent earthquake, and the hopelessness of passengers on a mighty ship passing to its watery grave. By reliving the events, the reader will see how disaster affects the lives of real people and will gain a deeper understanding of their sorrow, their pain, their courage, and their hope.

Introduction
A Disaster Without Parallel

What would happen today if an unknown disease mysteriously appeared in the United States and killed one or two — or even more — members of every American family? Imagine a plague so terrible that even if you survived, you would probably lose a brother or sister, a parent, or a grandparent.

Between the years 1347 and 1350, just such a terrible plague ravaged Europe. In four years, it killed approximately 25 million people, or one out of every three Europeans. There was scarcely a family that did not lose at least one member, and most families lost three or four.

In the cities hit worst by the plague, hundreds of people died every day. So many died that they could not be properly buried. Their bodies littered the streets. Survivors paid thieves and ruffians to carry the dead away and bury them. Loading the corpses on slabs of wood, these "pallbearers" carted the dead to the outskirts of town and dumped them into large pits.

This was the Black Death, the worst natural disaster in European history. The loss of life was staggering, and the damage was immense. In cities and villages across Europe, the Black Death disrupted anything that resembled routine daily life. Governments could not govern, and soldiers could not fight. In many cities, people roamed the streets, entered abandoned houses, and took whatever they pleased. They had little fear of getting caught, and most of them did not care. They believed that the world was coming to an end.

The people who lived through this horrible plague did not call it the Black Death. That name was first applied by historians a few centuries later. At the time, people called it "the pestilence," or simply, "the plague." Perhaps the worst part of it was that no one could explain the plague. Medieval philosophers speculated on its meaning, while physicians consulted their books of magic and astrology in search of a cure. They tried many treatments, but none of them worked.

Today we can understand scientifically what caused the Black Death. But it is difficult to comprehend just how devastating it was. In European history, the five hundred years before the Black Death are known as the Middle Ages, or the medieval period. During this entire period, life changed very little. The powerful traditions of the church and the nobility, or landholders, ruled people's lives.

A look at the people of the Middle Ages and the way they lived, will show how completely their lives were shattered by the Black Death. It destroyed the economy as well as traditional beliefs and loyalties. There was no returning to the way things had been for the past five hundred years. The Black Death brought an end to the Middle Ages.

The Black Death's Place in History

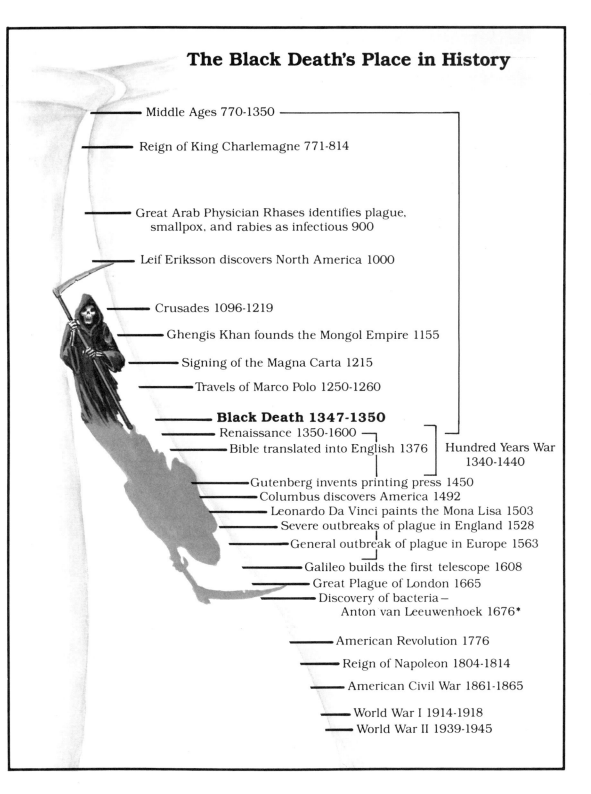

Middle Ages 770-1350

Reign of King Charlemagne 771-814

Great Arab Physician Rhases identifies plague, smallpox, and rabies as infectious 900

Leif Eriksson discovers North America 1000

Crusades 1096-1219

Ghengis Khan founds the Mongol Empire 1155

Signing of the Magna Carta 1215

Travels of Marco Polo 1250-1260

Black Death 1347-1350

Renaissance 1350-1600

Bible translated into English 1376

Hundred Years War 1340-1440

Gutenberg invents printing press 1450

Columbus discovers America 1492

Leonardo Da Vinci paints the Mona Lisa 1503

Severe outbreaks of plague in England 1528

General outbreak of plague in Europe 1563

Galileo builds the first telescope 1608

Great Plague of London 1665

Discovery of bacteria — Anton van Leeuwenhoek 1676*

American Revolution 1776

Reign of Napoleon 1804-1814

American Civil War 1861-1865

World War I 1914-1918

World War II 1939-1945

One
In a Medieval Village

In the English countryside in 1347, great stone castles stood on the tops of many hills. Around each castle was a small village. And in the castle lived the family and servants of the noble **lords** who ruled the village and the surrounding land as far as the eye could see.

Most of the people who lived in the villages were poor peasants. The crops they grew and the taxes they paid made their landlords rich. The small minority of wealthy landowners who lived in castles or big **manor** houses were known as the **nobility**.

Castles, which consisted of one or more buildings, were usually located on hills so they would not be easy to attack. War was a constant threat during the **Middle Ages**, and castles were built primarily for defense. They were usually enclosed by a huge stone wall, often more than 100 feet high (30 meters) and 20 feet thick (6 meters). Watchtowers rose even higher so that watchmen could see for miles in every direction. To make them even more difficult to penetrate, some castle walls were surrounded by a large ditch, or moat.

The wall was thick enough for people to walk on. When the castle was under attack, soldiers could run along the top of the thick wall, called a wall walk, and shoot arrows down at attackers.

Inside the castle wall was a large courtyard. The courtyard was always a busy place, full of knights, **squires** (young men training to become knights), noble women, maids, and servants. Peasants in the courtyard delivered supplies, carried messages, groomed horses, cleaned stables, tended the gardens, and worked on repairing the castle. From small shops around the yard, the clanging of blacksmiths' anvils and the pounding of carpenters' hammers could be heard.

The main building in the castle was the **keep**, a well-fortified structure with several towers and chambers. It may have looked impressive from the outside, but inside it was usually dark, smoky, damp, smelly, and generally uncomfortable. Windows in the keep were very narrow and let little light or air inside.

The first floor of the keep usually served as a dungeon, so the main entrance was on the second story, which could only be reached from a wall walk. This entry led to the great hall, the largest room in the keep. It was like a dining room, ballroom, and meeting room all in one. The great hall was several stories high, with stairways leading to the living and sleeping quarters.

The cold stone floors of the great hall were usually covered with straw. At mealtimes, people threw meat, bones, and other scraps on the straw for the dogs and cats. At night, servants slept on the straw.

Most castles consisted only of a keep. But the castles of dukes, earls, and other powerful noblemen, however, contained additional wings to house the families of knights, **courtiers**, or members of the court, and manor officials. In England, the **steward**, who managed the daily affairs of the manor, and the **bailiff**, who managed the lord's farms, often lived in the castle.

ENTERTAINING NOBLE GUESTS

When a lord invited other members of the nobility to his manor, it was important to treat the guests royally. He often gave a great feast and sponsored a **jousting tournament** for entertainment. The local peasants were expected to help make the preparations and provide the food for such events, and the costs could be staggering.

One visit from King Richard II of England to the Duke of Kent required that mountains of food be gathered by the villagers for the occasion: 120 sheep, 16 oxen, 152 pigs, 210 geese, 900 chickens, 12,000 pigeons, 50 swans, 11,000 eggs, and 130 gallons of milk and cream. The food gathered for the king's brief visit would have fed thousands of peasants for a full year.

The village, or manor, that surrounded the castle included twenty or thirty cottages made of sticks and mud, a small church, a blacksmith shop, a tavern, a mill, a bakery, and hundreds of narrow strips of farmland. A single dirt road ran through the village, connecting it with neighboring villages. Thousands of similar manors dotted the landscape of England and Europe. Seventy-five percent of the people lived in these medieval villages.

On his manor, the lord's word was the law. The peasants who lived there were his subjects, and few of them traveled far beyond the manor. Most of the peasants were **serfs**. They were legally bound to serve the manor for life. Historians call this kind of social organization **manorialism**.

Under this system, the noble lord provided his peasants with small strips of land to farm, and he protected them and their land from invaders. In return, the lord required the peasants to work for him two or three days a week, usually tending his farm. After completing this work, they could farm their own small strips of land. But the lord would take a part of their crops as taxes to pay for their defense.

Peasants could not leave the village without the lord's approval. They also needed his permission to clear new land or build a new hut. The lord rarely granted permission without demanding a tax. Villagers had to pay taxes to have their grain milled by the village miller, to get married, and even to bury their dead in the village churchyard.

Life for most villagers was short and difficult. A peasant family lived in a one-room hut that was cold, dark, and damp. Everyone slept in the same room, usually in wooden beds filled with straw. Most huts did not have fireplaces, so

the peasants built fires on the bare dirt floors. They were lucky if they had enough food to survive each winter, especially after paying the manor lord a portion of their crops for rent. Every winter many died of starvation, pneumonia, or other diseases caused by their poor living conditions.

Not all villagers were poor, however. The most important peasant on the manor was the **reeve**, a trusted peasant who worked for the lord as a kind of foreman, or working boss. The reeve was a person to be respected, and his family enjoyed a higher standard of living than the other peasants.

The reeve's cottage was bigger and better furnished than the others. It may have had oak tables and chairs, a chest filled with the family's best clothes, and even a long wooden bench for guests. The dirt floors may have been covered with straw mats.

The village also had a number of **freemen**, who were paid for their labor and were not bound to the manor for life. Most of them were skilled craftsmen who produced all the goods needed in the village. They usually passed their trade down from father to son. After a few generations, a family became known by the name of its craft. Every village had a Smith family, Miller family, Carpenter family, and Baker family. The Wheeler family made wheels for wagons. The Hayward family guarded the hay and livestock, and the Chandler family provided everyone with candles. During the Middle Ages, villages were so self-sufficient that villagers rarely had to leave to purchase anything they needed. In fact, few peasants ever ventured far beyond their own village, except perhaps to visit relatives in a neighboring village or to attend a fair in a nearby city.

THE FEALTY OATH

The medieval **fealty oath** spelled out the obligations of a less powerful lord, or **vassal**, and his superior, whom he addressed as "my lord." Every nobleman was a vassal to a more powerful nobleman. For example, a manor lord may have been the vassal of an earl. The earl, in turn, was vassal to a duke, who was the vassal of a king. The king, according to this system, was God's vassal.

The vassal promised to serve his lord loyally and defend him in battle whenever called upon. In return, his lord gave the vassal control over a piece of land called a **fief**. A fief could contain a single manor, or several manors, or even a hundred or more.

Every fief was part of a larger fief. The manor lord might have held a single manor, which was usually inherited from his father, who had inherited it from his father, and so on. Several manor lords all held fiefs within a larger fief that belonged to a more powerful lord, such as an earl. The manor lords were the earl's vassals. Many earls held fiefs within a still larger fief, which usually belonged to a duke. Finally, all the dukes' fiefs made up one large fief, called the kingdom. The kingdom was the king's fief. Supposedly, it had been granted to him by God.

When a king put out a call to arms or a demand for taxes, his dukes or other vassals responded. They passed the demand on to their vassals, who passed them down to their vassals, and so on down to the lowest ranking manor lords. These lords collected their taxes from their peasants.

Year after year and generation after generation, life in the village changed very little. **Inheritance** was extremely important to the **medieval** way of life. Peasants inherited family plots of land, and they also inherited their bondage to the manor lord.

Whenever a lord died, his firstborn son inherited his land and title of nobility. Titles such as king, prince, duke, earl, or lord indicated how much land and political power a nobleman had. Although the titles varied from country to country, land and political power always went hand-in-hand. Historians call this **feudalism**.

In a feudal society, no one really *owns* land. Instead, it is "held" through a chain of loyalty promises called **fealty oaths**. Each fealty oath is like a military alliance between two lords, one of whom is more powerful than the other.

Over the centuries, however, loyalties and fealty oaths often became quite confused. Several things happened to contribute to this. Noble families arranged marriages to create powerful alliances. Through inheritances, wars, rewards, bribes, and other influences, oaths changed and loyalties shifted. The social order in Europe became a confusing jumble of kings, princes, dukes, earls, counts, barons, and knights.

Quite often, two noblemen claimed the same land. Each one could cite a fealty oath that entitled him to it. Rival lords, from low-ranking knights to the mightiest kings, contested one another's land rights. Using their fealty oaths, they called upon their **vassals**, who were trained as knights. Vassals assembled armies of peasant foot soldiers, and together they defended their lords' loyalties and land rights. With this method

THE BATTLE

Most battles were an odd mixture of courtesy and savagery—part ceremony and part vicious combat. The battle usually began with great fanfare. Waving colorful banners and sounding its trumpets, a challenging army would present itself in front of a castle before laying *siege* to it. As village peasants hurried inside the castle walls, a knight from the attacking army rode forward to issue a ceremonial challenge.

The knight usually declared that he was fighting to defend the honor of a noble lady. Then an opposing knight emerged from the castle gate to accept this challenge. He declared his own loyalty to a noble lady for whom he was ready to lay down his life.

The two knights rode to an open field and fought, while members of both armies looked on.

Sometimes they fought on horseback, using *lances* and *maces*. Lowering their visors, the two would charge full speed at each other, trying to knock the other from his horse. At other times, knights fought on foot, swinging huge swords with both hands. A master swordsman could stab an opponent between two pieces of armor at the arm or leg joints.

The ceremony quickly turned to bloody combat. Every knight brought with him several peasants, who fought as foot soldiers. They wore little or no armor, and carried *halberds*, or axes, and *crossbows* as weapons. The foot soldiers marched in front of a cavalry of knights on horseback. They stormed castles and ransacked villages. While few knights actually died in battle, the casualties among foot soldiers were extremely high.

for settling disputes, noble lords were constantly at war in the Middle Ages.

Despite wars and rivalries, the feudal system helped hold medieval society together for hundreds of years. One strong supporter of the feudal system was the medieval church. The reason was simple: the church was probably the wealthiest and most powerful landlord in all of Europe.

Over the years, the church developed its own elaborate **hierarchy**. **Bishops** were like powerful lords. Every bishop was the highest religious authority in his region, or **diocese**. Some **archbishops** ruled over several bishops, and the **pope**, or bishop of Rome, was given authority over them all. Below the bishops were **abbots**, or directors of monasteries. Below them were the **monks** and the village priests. Monks usually enjoyed a comfortable lifestyle in their monasteries, and some became quite wealthy. Village priests were usually poor like the rest of the peasants.

The church's income came from many sources. First, every medieval family was expected to pay the church a **tithe**, or a tenth of its earnings. Although the village priest collected these tithes and other gifts, he kept little for himself or the village church. The rest he sent to the abbots and bishops from whom he took his orders.

The church also received gifts of land and money from wealthy noblemen who wanted to guarantee their salvation. Over the years, the church acquired a great deal of land, and bishops and abbots became major landowners. Just like other lords, they had farms to tend, villages to govern, fealty oaths to honor, and vassals to serve them.

Along with the land came political power, and appointments to many positions in the church were based more on political loyalties than religious qualifications. In fact, members of some noble families became priests just to qualify for these positions.

In the Middle Ages, priests and other church leaders taught that the power of the nobility and the poverty of the peasants was part of God's plan. God had arranged all living and non-living things in a perfect hierarchy. People, for example, could be divided into three distinct classes, or three "for alls." There were lords who "ruled for all," priests who "prayed for all," and peasants who "worked for all." As long as people accepted their station in life and did what was expected of them, they were assured of an eternal life in heaven. For such eternal happiness, peasants were willing to accept their short, wretched lives on earth.

They rarely questioned their lowly status because they saw only what the church and the nobility wanted them to see. For nearly five centuries, what most peasants saw was lords living in great houses and bishops serving glorious cathedrals. They heard priests speaking in Latin, a language they did not understand, and they saw noble ladies dressed in rich silks. These people seemed superior to them in every way.

The power of the church and the strength of the feudal system gave society the law and order it needed. With

this kind of stability, the population of Europe grew steadily. In the ninth century, only about thirty million people lived in Europe. By 1347, that number had grown to about sixty million.

That many people, however, created new problems for medieval society. Many landlords had more peasants on their land than they could manage. Unwilling to sacrifice any of their own wealth, they could not divide the peasants' farms into enough pieces to provide a decent living for everyone.

They put peasants to work cutting down forests and clearing new land. But they could not do it fast enough. One consequence of this land shortage was that noblemen began to offer vassals, craftsmen, and even peasants, money instead of land for their services.

Many peasants were squeezed into smaller and smaller pieces of land. Some who had managed to save a little money decided to run away from their villages and look for work elsewhere. By 1347, few lords tried to stop their peasants from leaving because there were too many people living on their manors as it was.

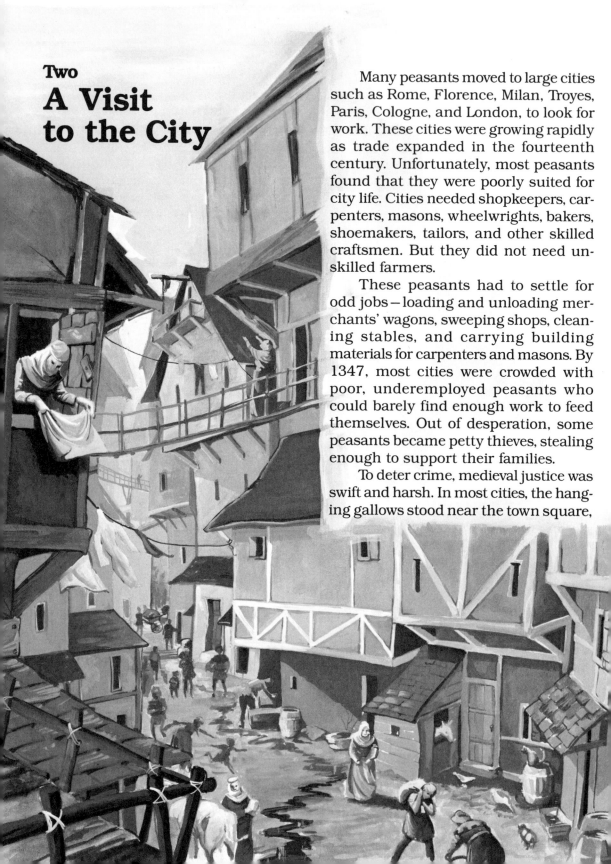

Two
A Visit to the City

Many peasants moved to large cities such as Rome, Florence, Milan, Troyes, Paris, Cologne, and London, to look for work. These cities were growing rapidly as trade expanded in the fourteenth century. Unfortunately, most peasants found that they were poorly suited for city life. Cities needed shopkeepers, carpenters, masons, wheelwrights, bakers, shoemakers, tailors, and other skilled craftsmen. But they did not need unskilled farmers.

These peasants had to settle for odd jobs—loading and unloading merchants' wagons, sweeping shops, cleaning stables, and carrying building materials for carpenters and masons. By 1347, most cities were crowded with poor, underemployed peasants who could barely find enough work to feed themselves. Out of desperation, some peasants became petty thieves, stealing enough to support their families.

To deter crime, medieval justice was swift and harsh. In most cities, the hanging gallows stood near the town square,

CRIME AND PUNISHMENT IN THE MIDDLE AGES

There were three levels of justice in the Middle ages. **High justice** was administered by the nobility. In their castles, noble lords tried people for murder, rape, armed robbery, treason, and other serious crimes. Anyone convicted of these crimes was sentenced to hang.

Ecclesiastical justice was administered by church officials. They tried people for crimes against the church, such as **heresy** and witchcraft. Anyone found guilty was sentenced to burn at the stake.

Finally, **civic courts** were held in city halls, where mayors and other city officials tried people for petty crimes, such as minor theft, cheating in the marketplace, or spreading gossip. Since there were no public prisons, first-time thieves were often placed in the **pillories** for several days. More serious offenders might be branded on the forehead with a hot iron. A judge might sentence a thief to lose a finger or even a whole hand. And there was

little tolerance for repeat offenders—they were usually hanged.

For lesser crimes, the punishment was usually public humiliation. Anyone convicted of spreading gossip could be sentenced to three dunks in a dunking stool. A baker accused of using rotten fish in his fish pies might be locked in a pillory for several hours, while the townspeople threw the rotten pies at his face.

and whenever there was a hanging, large crowds gathered to watch. Dead bodies were often left dangling for several days as a grim warning to those who might be tempted by a life of crime.

As cities continued to grow, so did crime and other problems of overcrowding. Since a city was usually enclosed by walls, more and more houses had to be packed into narrow, winding streets. Three- or four-story stucco houses, painted in shades of red, green, and blue, stood one right next to the other. Some were built like triangles to fit on street corners. Others had even stranger shapes to fit wherever space was available. Many houses had small first floors and larger upper stories that jutted out above the street.

Usually, two or three families shared a single floor in one of these damp, dark houses. When night fell, the houses were pitch dark because most people could

not afford to burn wood. The windows of these houses had no glass. Most did not even have wooden shutters. Instead, they were covered with cloth or perhaps wool blankets for extra insulation in the winter.

Cows and pigs were kept in stables attached to almost every house. In the muddy streets, flocks of geese fluttered to avoid horsedrawn wagons, while children in rough wool breeches and simple smocks shouted and played.

Only the main streets in most cities were paved. Most of the streets were just dirt paths wide enough for a single cart to drive on. Even on sunny days, they remained muddy because the houses blocked most of the sunlight. Crude pipes carried human waste from the houses down to the streets. There garbage and other waste lay rotting in the gutters, where dogs, cats, pigs, and rats searched for food.

The medieval city was a place of great contrasts. And the dark, muddy streets, where most residents lived, contrasted dramatically with the cobblestone streets near the city center, where merchants and **master** craftsmen carried on their thriving business.

On market days, the heart of the city was like a carnival. With a deafening ring, the pealing of church bells announced the opening of the market. Merchants and craftsmen stood in colorful tents and wooden stalls, selling food, clothing, saddles, knives, swords, jewelry, and other products. Crowds gathered around jugglers, wrestlers, and dancing bears.

Walking through the streets, the **town crier** rang a small handbell as he recited official news. Merchants, dressed in colorful, finely embroidered coats and hats, bartered and bickered among themselves. Peasants loaded and unloaded merchandise on merchants' wagons.

The smells of freshly baked breads, meatpies, and other foods drifted from nearby shops. The pleasant aroma, however, could not cover the smells of manure and human waste.

Along the cobblestone streets were the homes of merchants and master craftsmen. Most of these were typical stucco houses. The ground floor usually contained a shop, while the upper stories housed the owner's family, servants, and **apprentices**.

A few of the houses were impressive structures made of bricks and stones. These belonged to the wealthiest bankers and businessmen in the city. Many merchant families had become more rich and powerful than the local nobility. Though their houses were not as big

as castles, they were often more comfortable. Today, many of these merchant houses are over seven hundred years old and still in use.

Most business streets had names such as Baker Street, Weaver Street, or Shoemaker Street. Almost every shop on Baker Street was a bakery, and the shops on Shoemaker Street were all shoe shops. Hanging above the front door outside most shops was a brass **guild** sign identifying the owner as a member of a local guild.

Almost every craft and business in the medieval city was controlled by a guild. These organizations played an important role in the life of the city. People could not practice a trade unless they belonged to one. Guild members regulated wages, prices, and standards of quality for their goods. They decided who could be an apprentice.

Craftsmen did not think of other members of their guild as competitors. One bakery owner, for instance, did not compete with another. Both would charge the same price for their bread, pay the same wages for their help, and assure the same quality for their customers. Both shop owners wanted to guarantee the success of all their guild members. They wanted to make sure they received a fair price for their products. And in city affairs, they wanted the interests of all bakers to be represented. In many cities, guilds controlled the town council.

For these and other reasons, most members lived and worked near their guild hall. They took great pride in their membership. They hung guild signs in front of their shops and often wore only certain colors so that everyone in town knew what guild they belonged to.

BUILDING A CATHEDRAL

Building a cathedral, which normally took more than a century to complete, required the work of **master** craftsmen from many guilds. The first year of construction was spent digging the hole for the foundation. As the first stones were laid in place, the architect, or master builder, would probably be there with an **apprentice**, possibly his own son. He would show the apprentice how important it was to make the foundation perfectly straight so that the walls of the cathedral would be strong.

After about a quarter of a century, the master builder would be ready to retire and hand the job over to his apprentice. If everything had gone well during his years of supervision, the main walls and **buttresses** might be half finished before he retired.

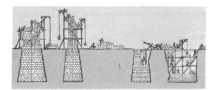

Foundations

Work on a cathedral was frequently interrupted for years at a time. The **diocese** might run out of money, or the whole city might stop to fight a war. With luck, the second master builder might live to see the walls and buttresses completed and work begun on the roof.

Finally, after a century or more of construction that spanned the careers of three or four master builders, the finished cathedral was dedicated to the glory of God. As the people stood inside, their sights would be drawn up to the vaulted ceiling

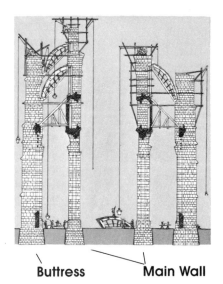

Buttress   **Main Wall**

high above and to the multi-colored windows with sunlight streaming through. As their eyes turned toward heaven, the worshipers may have thought about all the workers over the years who had built the cathedral. They may have thought particularly of those who had been killed while working on it.

In most cities, by 1347, guilds held more political power than the nobility. The church, however, was still the most powerful institution in the city. One look at the city's skyline made that clear. Reaching higher than the other buildings in town were the spires and steeples of all its churches. Most spectacular of all was the cathedral, which towered over the city. This monstrous structure often took more than a century to build.

Though building a cathedral cost the church dearly, nothing contributed more to a city's pride than a great cathedral. And the massive construction project was a great boost to the economy. It attracted architects, stone masons, carpenters, glass makers, and other craftsmen from miles around. The craftsmen hired thousands of peasants to work for them. Local blacksmiths were flooded with demands for tools. Business also increased for shoemakers, tailors, leather tanners, bakers, butchers, and other merchants.

People traveling to find work in the cities were joined on the road by merchants. In January 1348, many merchants were on the winter fair circuit, traveling to major trade fairs in such cities as Florence, Siena, Lyons, and Troyes. At night, these travelers gathered in inns along the major trade routes. There they swapped news, gossip, and stories of the road.

A typical medieval inn was just an ordinary four-story house. The first floor was a tavern, and the second was reserved for guests who needed a place to spend the night. The innkeeper, his family, and his servants occupied the upper stories.

In the tavern, waitresses scooped

wine and ale out of barrels and into pewter mugs. These they served to the guests, who sat on wooden benches and three-legged stools. Travelers were easy to spot in the crowd because they had mud caked on their boots and cloaks. Local citizens also came to the tavern to hear news from the outside world. Bakers, shoemakers, physicians, a few scholars, and even a priest or two sat listening to the merchants' descriptions of far-off lands.

The news that Italian merchants brought to these inns in 1348 was extremely disturbing. In hushed voices, they spoke of a terrible **pestilence**, or disease, that was sweeping through the cities of Italy. The entire tavern would grow silent as merchants described the horror that had befallen the rich, beautiful city of Florence.

Once a center of banking and the textile industry, Florence was now in chaos. As many as a thousand people a day were dying, and their bodies littered the streets. Many of Florence's most prominent citizens fled from the city. As accounts of Florence spread, people throughout Europe began to speak of the disease as the "Florentine Plague."

When curious listeners asked the merchants where this terrible disease had come from, they responded with their versions of the story of Messina, a busy port city on the Italian island of Sicily.

Three
Merchants of Death

In October of 1347, a fleet of twelve merchant ships sailed from Caffa, a Middle Eastern port on the Black Sea, toward Messina. They were Genoese merchant ships, and they were stopping in Messina before returning to their home port in Genoa, Italy.

The people of Messina always waited excitedly for ships from the Middle East. They were eager to see the exotic silks, rugs, perfumes, and spices that merchants usually brought with them. Instead of their usual cargo, however, these ships carried something

strange and terrible which would change the lives of people in Messina forever.

Citizens who lined the shore noticed something strange even before the ships docked. Each of the large vessels, which usually had a crew of about forty men, was swerving crazily back and forth. As the ships drew closer to port, people on the shore could see that each one was manned by only six or seven sailors.

When the ships finally docked at Messina, local officials went aboard to see what was wrong. As soon as they stepped on board, they were struck by the overpowering smell of decaying bodies. Dying people lay helplessly on the decks. Their bodies were covered with large, black swellings, or **buboes**. Most of the crew and passengers on all twelve ships had died from the horrible pestilence and been buried at sea.

City officials feared that the disease might spread to their city. They issued an order that no person or piece of merchandise was to leave the Genoese ships. The officials did not know what caused this terrible disease, but they wanted nothing to do with it. They even forbade medical treatment to sick sailors and passengers.

Where had this terrible disease come from? Apparently, Genoese merchants and their families who were living in Caffa had been exposed to it during the summer of 1347. That summer Tatars, or Mongolian warriors, attacked the Genoese in Caffa. They surrounded the city and trapped the Genoese inside for several months.

Just when they seemed on the verge of victory, however, the Tatars suffered an unexpected blow. An outbreak of plague wiped out most of their army, and they were forced to retreat. According to legend, the angry Tatars believed that the disease was a curse from the Genoese. In revenge, they catapulted the corpses of plague victims over the city wall into Caffa.

While we do not know whether this is true, thanks to monks and other record keepers of the day, known as **chroniclers**, we have a vivid picture of how the Black Death spread. It began to spread in Caffa shortly after the Tatars retreated. The Genoese soon realized that their best hope for survival was to leave Caffa at once. So they boarded their twelve merchant vessels and sailed for Italy.

When they left Caffa, no one on board had any symptoms of the plague. Slowly, however, it crept upon them, first on one ship then another. By the time the fleet reached Messina, plague had infected three-fourths of the people on the ships. Passengers who had the strength to stand were pressed into service.

Women and children had to help raise and lower the sails.

For two days, these ships sat at the port in Messina. After the inspection by city officials, no one went aboard, and nothing came ashore, except for a few rats that had been on the ships since Caffa. They scampered down the ropes to the dock and disappeared into the city. Finally, the Genoese fleet and its tiny crew set sail for Genoa.

A few days later, several people in Messina fell sick. Even though they had tried to prevent it, city officials had been unable to stop the plague. Once people caught it, nothing could be done for them. And once the disease gained a foothold, there was no stopping it.

In two months, nearly half the people in Messina died. Worse yet, the plague spread to other cities in Italy, and it seemed to follow the same routes used by most medieval merchants. Soon Genoa, Venice, and other ports on the Italian peninsula were struck by plague. In early spring, the plague moved inland to Rome, Florence, Siena, and other cities on the major trade routes. By the spring of 1348, it had killed almost half of the people in Italy's major cities.

MEDIEVAL TRADE ROUTES

Trade between Europe and the Orient followed a cycle. Merchants from Venice and Genoa sailed east on the Mediterranean Sea to Constantinople, Caffa, and other cities on the Black Sea. They brought tools, metals, wool, linen, and lumber from Europe. These they traded to Eastern merchants for silks, spices, carpets, and other oriental products. Then merchants returned to Europe and sold their oriental cargo in such Mediterranean ports as Marseilles, Valencia, Genoa, and Venice.

Other merchants bought the exotic oriental products at these ports, and transported them into Italy, Spain, France, Germany, and England. They sold them in these countries in order to buy more tools, metals, wool, linen, and lumber. Then the trade cycle would start all over again.

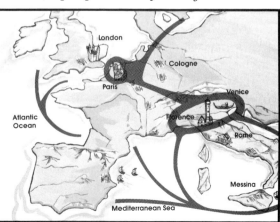

The Black Death did not stop there. In January 1348, a chronicler in the French port of Marseilles reported the arrival of another Genoese merchant ship carrying sick and dying passengers. A few crew members actually came ashore in Marseilles before horrified authorities ordered them back to their ship and demanded that the ship depart at once.

But it was too late. Within weeks Marseilles and other French ports along the Mediterranean Sea had been overrun by plague. In the summer of 1348, the plague reached Paris. At the time, Paris had a reputation as the most learned city in the world. It had one of the oldest universities in Europe, and its Faculty of Medicine had trained more physicians than any other university.

Yet Parisians were no more successful at combating the plague than anyone else had been. Here is an eyewitness report from the Hotel Dieu, the central hospital in Paris:

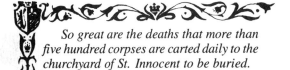

So great are the deaths that more than five hundred corpses are carted daily to the churchyard of St. Innocent to be buried.

Several of the city's highest ranking churchmen and nobility died from the plague, but many fled to the country. That left the city with no one in control. Unruly mobs terrorized the poor and sick. They broke into houses and shops, with little fear of being arrested.

Meanwhile, a few miles from the city, wealthy families waited for the disease to pass. While they ate, drank, and entertained themselves in the countryside, some troubled Parisians criticized them for abandoning the city. One citizen, Jean Paul Papon, wrote:

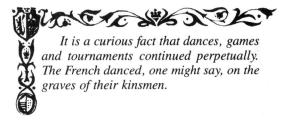

It is a curious fact that dances, games and tournaments continued perpetually. The French danced, one might say, on the graves of their kinsmen.

Even in the countryside, people were not safe for long. One chronicler, Gilles Li Musis, reported in the summer of 1348 that misery had begun to spread to the country villages:

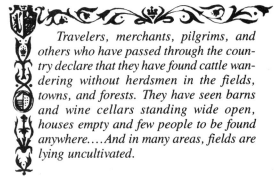

Travelers, merchants, pilgrims, and others who have passed through the country declare that they have found cattle wandering without herdsmen in the fields, towns, and forests. They have seen barns and wine cellars standing wide open, houses empty and few people to be found anywhere....And in many areas, fields are lying uncultivated.

From Paris, the disease spread in two main directions—east toward Germany, and north toward England.

In northern France, English soldiers witnessed the plague during the fall of 1348. England and France were at war with each other, and the English had captured much of northern France. So soldiers sailing back to England in 1348 carried reports of a terrible disease that was killing thousands of French people. They probably believed that this was a good punishment for the French, who had dared to challenge the English king, Edward III.

Little did the English soldiers suspect that even as they were sharing their stories of disease, it was beginning to spread among them. By spring of 1349, officials in London were trying to stop the Black Death from repeating what it had already done in so many other cities.

Officials restricted travel, banned outsiders, and **quarantined** victims of the plague. All ships from the Mediterranean were denied entry to the harbor. Travelers were stopped and questioned at city gates, and anyone who looked suspicious or ill was turned away. Some townspeople even sealed up the homes of their afflicted neighbors, condemning everyone inside, sick and healthy alike, to certain death. But still the plague crept into their city.

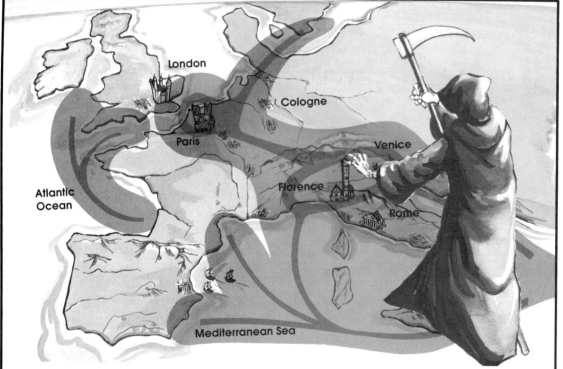

THE PATH OF THE BLACK DEATH

From 1347 through 1350, what we now call the Black Death made its deadly march across Europe. By the end of 1348, it had reached the north coast of France. A year later, it crossed the English Channel and engulfed most of England, Ireland, and Scotland. In 1350, it completed its devastation by sweeping through Germany, Holland, Denmark, Norway, Sweden, and Finland.

The plague followed the same major sea and land routes that merchants used. It reached the Black Sea from China. From there it came by sea to several Mediterranean ports.

Traveling overland, it hit the great trade centers of Italy and France. One after another, the cities of Lyons, Troyes, Provins, Paris, and Ghent fell to the Black Death. From each of these cities, it spread in every direction until it engulfed almost every city, town, and village in France and Belgium.

From France, the disease took two main routes. One fork advanced the **epidemic** northward to London and throughout England, Ireland, and Scotland. The second fork followed the overland trade route from Paris to Cologne. Once it reached this German city, the Black Death took an eastward land route to Hamburg and a northward sea route into Denmark, Norway, and Sweden.

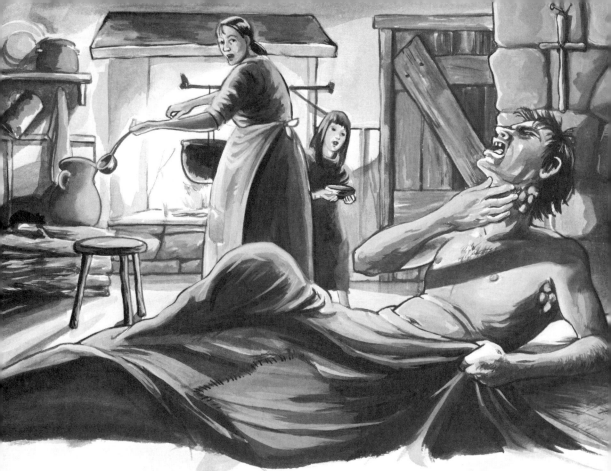

When victims caught the plague, their first symptoms were the painful swellings, or buboes, that most commonly appeared in the armpits and the groin area. These swellings often got as big as an egg and sometimes as large as an orange. In addition to the buboes, dark blisters and purplish blotches appeared on the skin. These symptoms were accompanied by a fever, severe headaches, increasing weakness, and usually death.

Every day the disease became increasingly painful. Delirious with pain and fever, some victims lost their sanity. They would suddenly strike out at someone, throw themselves out of windows, plunge into a river, or run naked through the streets until they collapsed. Most people who caught the disease

lived less than a week.

When the plague struck a city or village, the number of deaths usually rose steadily for several weeks. Then the disease would go away as mysteriously as it had arrived. In a few cities and villages, that was the end of the tragedy. People grieved over the loss of loved ones, and life returned to normal.

In most cities, however, just when things seemed to be returning to normal, a second phase of the plague would strike. Often it was worse than the first—and more mysterious. Many people died even though they did not have any buboes or dark blotches on their skin. Their only signs of illness were extreme weakness, a continuous fever, and coughing up blood. According to one medieval physician, as soon as he saw a patient coughing blood, he knew there was no hope:

Anyone who is infected by it dies. All who see him in his sickness, or visit him, or do any business with him, or even carry him to the grave, quickly follow him there, and there is no known means of protection.

In this phase, the plague spread with mystifying speed. At least one physician believed, quite seriously, that looks could kill:

Instantaneous death occurs when the spirit, escaping from the eyes of the sick man, strikes the eyes of a healthy person standing near. This happens especially when the onlooker is in agony. For then the poisonous nature of the disease passes swiftly from one to the other.

In most cities and villages, the death toll grew steadily for months. The shadow of the Black Death touched every person in Europe. Almost every family lost loved ones. Parents buried their children. Children who had lost their parents, grandparents, aunts, and uncles wandered through cities trying to find a familiar face or a crumb to eat.

After a few months in one city or village, the plague would go away. But it would soon reappear in a nearby town. In this manner, the Black Death moved from town to town between 1347 and 1350. In most places, it killed a third, a half, or even a larger share of the population. Terrified, people waited helplessly as the dark shadow of the Black Death spread across Europe.

Four
Beneath
the Shadow

Historians are constantly examining and adjusting the story of the past. They pore over letters, official documents, church and family records. From this process, they attempt to piece together an accurate picture of our past.

Often missing from this picture is an understanding of how people living at the time reacted to the events that we call history. Only eyewitness accounts, written by people who actually experienced these events, can give us this information. In the case of the Black Death, several eyewitnesses tell us what it was like to live while the plague raged around them.

It is a rare fortune to have such vivid accounts of the past. But even more rare is an account written by one of the most important writers in Western literature. The Italian writer Giovanni Boccaccio lived in Florence at the time of the plague. In the preface to his most famous work, *the Decameron*, he describes the events in that city so vividly it is as if we are witnessing the Black Death as it happens.

Boccaccio begins his account by describing the symptoms that afflicted most victims:

At the onset of the disease, both men and women were afflicted by a sort of swelling in the groin or under the arms which sometimes reached the size of a common apple or egg. Some of these swellings were larger and some smaller, and all were commonly called boils. From these two starting points the boils began in a little while to spread and appear generally all over the body.

As a member of a prominent Florentine family, Boccaccio could observe people from all classes. Some thought that the best way to avoid the disease was to exercise extreme caution. Others took the opposite view. They believed that they were powerless against the plague. So they did just as they pleased, living every day as though it were their last:

> Some among them believed that by living temperately and guarding against excess of all kinds, they could help avoid the danger. Forming a band, they lived away from the rest of the world.
>
> Others held that plenty of drinking and enjoyment, singing and free living in every possible way was the best way to avoid the disease. Day and night they went from one tavern to another drinking and carousing unrestrainedly.
>
> They ran wild in other people's houses. And there was no one to prevent them, for everyone had abandoned all responsibility for their belongings, considering their days numbered. Consequently, most of the houses had become common property, and strangers would make use of them at will. Following this way of thinking, they did their best to run away from the infected.

One reason for such chaos and abuse of the law was that most sheriffs and ministers of justice had died or abandoned their duties:

> Even the authority of divine and human law had crumbled and fallen into decay. For its ministers and executors, like other men, had either died or sickened, or had been left so entirely without assistants that they were unable to attend to their duties. As a result, everyone had free rein to do as he saw fit.

Boccaccio may have been among the few members of the privileged class who stayed in the city. His description of sickness and death in the streets suggests that he observed the full horror of the Black Death in Florence. He estimates that between March and the following July, more than 100,000 people lost their lives within the walls of Florence.

Death was so common that one funeral procession seemed to follow another. For their own sanity, people learned to ignore these processions or even to make fun of them. Indeed, the processions were often a strange sight. Sometimes the dead were not accompanied by friends and relatives but by rough-looking grave diggers who were paid to attend:

> *Laughter, jest, and carousing accompanied the dead. Even naturally compassionate women had learned this for their health's sake. It was rare for a corpse to be followed to church by more than ten or twelve mourners. And these were not the usual respectable citizens, but a class of vulgar grave diggers who called themselves "**sextons**" and did these services for a price.*
>
> *They crept under the **bier** and shouldered it, and then with hasty steps rushed it to the nearest churchyard. Usually they walked behind five or six members of the clergy, with little light and sometimes with none at all. Then, with the help of these "sextons," the priests lowered the dead into the first unoccupied grave they came across.*

The plague claimed the lives of both rich and poor, but not equally. When the plague reached its peak in Florence, many of the wealthy escaped to their castles and villas in the country:

> *Still others maintained that the best remedy against the plague was to leave it miles behind. Men and women without number, caring for nobody but themselves, abandoned the city, their houses and estates, their own flesh and blood even, and their belongings, in search of a country place—it made no difference whether it were their own or their neighbor's.*

Poor and middle-class people had no such hope of escape. Soon the streets were filled with the stench of their dying bodies:

More wretched still were the circumstances of the common people and, for a great part, of the middle class. Confined to their homes and restricted to their sections of the city, they fell sick daily by the thousands. There, without help or care, they died almost without exception. A great many breathed their last in the public streets, day and night. A large number perished in their homes, and it was only by the stench of their decaying bodies that they proclaimed their death to their neighbors. Everywhere the city was teeming with corpses.

THE PLAGUE MAIDEN

Many people believed the cause of the plague was a beautiful but evil witch called the "plague maiden." It was said that when she passed by a house she could infect those inside simply by waving a red scarf through an open window or door.

According to Austrian legend, however, one man saved his village by stealing the maiden's scarf. He deliberately left his window open and waited with his sword drawn for the maiden to arrive. As she thrust the feared red scarf in the window, the brave villager chopped off her hand. He was the last in his village to die from the plague.

Boccaccio goes on to describe how most of these peasants and common people were buried:

They would drag the corpses out of their homes and pile them in front of the doors, where every morning, countless bodies could be seen. The dead were laid upon ordinary boards, two or three at once. It was not unusual to see a single bier carrying husband and wife, two or three brothers, father and son, and others besides.

When a couple of priests were walking, carrying a cross before a corpse, they were soon followed by two or three sets of "sextons." And where the holy men had thought to be burying one man, they found seven or eight on their hands, sometimes more. Death had become so common that no more attention was given to human lives than would be given to goats brought to slaughter.

So many bodies were brought to the churches every day that the burial grounds could not hold them. Huge trenches were dug in the crowded churchyards and the dead were piled in them, layer upon layer, like merchandise in the hold of a ship. A little earth covered the corpses of each row, and the procedure continued until the trench was filled to the top.

In Siena, a city not far from Florence, chronicler Agnola di Turi recorded the similar fate of that city. Before the plague, Siena held a reputation as a center for learning and the arts. Then came the Black Death. Unlike Florence, Siena was never able to recover its prominent position among European cities. Its famous school of art closed its doors for good. The words of Agnola di Turi show how the plague changed hope to hopelessness for many in Siena:

Out of fear, people turned their backs on the sick, on one another, and even on their own families:

The calamity had instilled such horror into the hearts of men and women that brother abandoned brother, uncles, sisters and wives left their dear ones to perish and, what is almost incredible, parents avoided visiting or nursing their very children, as though these were not their own flesh.

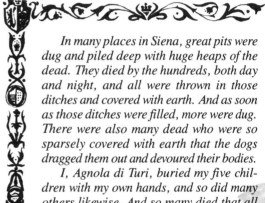

In many places in Siena, great pits were dug and piled deep with huge heaps of the dead. They died by the hundreds, both day and night, and all were thrown in those ditches and covered with earth. And as soon as those ditches were filled, more were dug. There were also many dead who were so sparsely covered with earth that the dogs dragged them out and devoured their bodies.

I, Agnola di Turi, buried my five children with my own hands, and so did many others likewise. And so many died that all believed it was the end of the world.

As the plague moved northward, it also spread from cities to villages. Very few villagers were able to read and write, so written accounts of the Black Death in the villages of Europe are sparse.

The most complete records were kept by monasteries and village churches in England. Fortunately, the account of William of Deve, a monk at St. Alban's **Monastery** in southern England, has survived. From them we can piece together an accurate story of what happened to the village of St. Alban's Manor. The events that took place in this village in March, 1349 were probably similar to those that occurred in villages throughout Europe. The villagers of St. Alban's Manor were glad to see spring arrive in 1349. After a hard winter, it was time for plowing and planting their fields and tending the farm of their manor lord.

The lord of the manor was Abbot Michael of Mentmore, the director of St. Alban's **Abbey** and Monastery. Judging from the monastery record of taxes, the abbot ran his manor in the traditional way. The majority of villagers were bonded to the manor for life.

On Thursday, March 30, 1349, vil-lagers brought food and gifts to the abbey to prepare for Easter Sunday. The abbot himself officiated at a special high mass. Just three days later, on Easter Sunday, he became the village's first victim of the Black Death. William of Deve has left this account of the abbot's death:

*The Abbot was the first to suffer from the dread disease, which was later to carry off his monks. He began to feel the first symptoms on **Maundy Thursday**, but out of reverence for the festival and remembering our Lord's humility, he celebrated High Mass, and then, before taking his dinner, humbly and devoutly washed the feet of the poor.*

*After he had taken his dinner he proceeded to wash and kiss the feet of all the monks and to carry out all the offices of the day alone and without assistance. The next day, when his sickness became worse, he took to his bed and, as a true Catholic, made his confession with a contrite heart and received the sacrament of **extreme unction**. Amidst the sorrow of all who surrounded him, he endured until noon on Easter Sunday.*

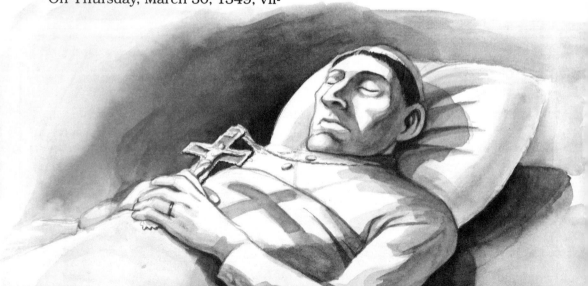

The abbot's death probably spread fear through the village. Why, people may have wondered, had God done this to one of his most faithful servants? Was it possible that the abbot had died for their sins so the rest of the village might be spared?

Any hope of being spared quickly disappeared. According to William of Deve, 47 monks died at the monastery within weeks after the abbot's death. Another abbot was assigned to St. Alban's but he, too, died of plague. Soon the entire monastery was abandoned.

Villagers at St. Alban's Manor planted no fields that spring. In the weeks that followed the abbot's death, few villagers even ventured out of their homes. Perhaps they hoped to avoid the disease by avoiding contact with their neighbors. Nevertheless, one-third of the people in the village died of the plague within two months.

Throughout Europe, in villages like St. Alban's Manor, people felt helpless as the pestilence crept steadily into their streets and homes. Their mud and stick huts became infirmaries for the sick and dying. Unlike the cities, these villages had no physicians to help them treat the dread disease and no philosophers to help them understand it.

Five
Searching for Answers

Medieval physicians and philosophers were of little help in the time of the plague. They did not understand the causes of **infectious diseases** or how they spread. Most explanations were based on folklore, superstition, and rumor. Blame was frequently placed on travelers and other suspicious outsiders. In cities across Europe, one group was singled out for blame more than any other: the Jewish community.

One practice that aroused great suspicion of Jews was their habit of drawing water from country springs rather than from city wells. They did this in keeping with traditional Jewish rules

of cleanliness, but some people immediately suspected them of poisoning the public wells. Reports circulated that Jews had been seen dropping mysterious vials or pouches into city wells. And when other Jews refused to drink from these wells, they were accused of conspiracy and tried in local courts.

On September 21, 1348, the city of Zurich voted never to admit Jews into their city again. In Basel, Switzerland, Jews were rounded up, forced into wooden buildings, and burned alive. The persecution was even worse in Germany, where hundreds of Jews were burned at the stake.

Most educated people denounced the slaughter, pointing out that Jewish people were dying of the plague, too. The pope also condemned the persecution, promising all Jews safe refuge in the churches of Europe.

The church is where most people turned first in troubled times. But during the Black Death, the church did not offer much comfort. It said that the plague was God's punishment.

What could the entire population of Europe, including kings, priests, paupers, children, and newborn infants, have done to incur such wrath? Perhaps it was the greed of the noble lords, the immodesty of women, or the laziness of peasants. Churchmen were quick to condemn the popularity of gambling and excessive drinking. Others argued that greed and disloyalty within the church itself had made God angry. Although a few innocent individuals may have had to suffer for the sins of others, most people found many reasons to feel guilty.

With that in mind, the first step toward stopping the plague had nothing to do with medicine, doctors, or treating the sick. The first course of action was to confess all sins and pray for forgiveness.

Unfortunately, these measures seemed to have little effect. Some people felt that more desperate actions were needed to persuade God to forgive them. They joined a movement that came to be known as the *flagellants*.

Most flagellants would walk from city to city in processions of two or three hundred, and sometimes as many as a thousand strong. As word traveled ahead, church bells would begin to ring, and the townsfolk poured out to welcome them. Each of the flagellants carried a **scourge**, a wooden stick with three or four leather tongs attached to one end. At the end of each tong was a sharp iron spike about an inch long.

With these scourges, they practiced *flagellation*, or self-beatings. Forming a huge circle in the center of town, they stripped to the waist and piled their garments in the middle of the circle.

Singing and chanting, they called on the townspeople to join them in repenting their sins. The flagellants marched around the circle, flailing their scourges and beating themselves on their backs and chests until they drew blood. Their leader walked among the crowd, urging everyone to pray for mercy. As blood trickled down the arms and chests of the flagellants, they increased the pace and intensity of their beatings, often falling into a state of hypnotic frenzy. It was not uncommon for one or two among them to drop dead in the middle of a ceremony.

The flagellants usually stayed in a town for two or three days, performing their ceremony at least once a day. By the time they left, they had usually convinced a few of the local residents to join them.

Unfortunately, their efforts did nothing to stop the spread of plague. Mysteriously, it seemed to get worse in places where the flagellants had been.

Learned men and women tried to find more logical explanations for the plague. Most of them shared the theory that it was carried by a mysterious "poisonous cloud" gradually moving across Europe. In fact, many claimed that they had seen the dark cloud hovering on the southern horizon.

It seemed logical to prevent the plague from spreading by burning fragrant leaves and herbs to purify the air. While this may have improved the smell of the garbage-filled medieval city and helped cover up the horrible stench of decaying bodies, it did nothing to stop the plague.

Others turned to physicians for advice. The practice of medicine in the Middle Ages was based on astrology, religion, and the philosophical writings of a third-century Greek physician named Galen. Galen's methods fit nicely with the medieval belief that disease was like sin. One was a corruption of the soul, the other a corruption of the body.

Just as a priest tried to drive evil from the soul, the doctor sought to drive illness from the body. Unfortunately, the methods used to drive out illness had little to do with scientific observation.

The most common method was **bloodletting**. Physicians believed they could drain the illness out with the blood. First they consulted astrological charts that told them how the stars were affecting various parts of the body. Then they cut into their patient's arm or leg and let the wound bleed.

At other times, physicians would try to accomplish the same thing by lancing the festering buboes directly. The blood that emerged from the buboes was not only thick and black, but it also gave off a foul smell. If a green scum appeared in the blood, the physician could do nothing but shake his head, knowing that it was too late for any treatment. Knowing nothing about sterilization or the spreading of germs, physicians often used the same scalpel on several patients.

The widely respected Arab physician Ibn Khatimah wrote that the critical secret to curing the plague was timing the lancing of the buboes just right. "One could halt the flow of the poison," he said, "if the buboes were operated upon between the fourth and seventh days of the disease, when the

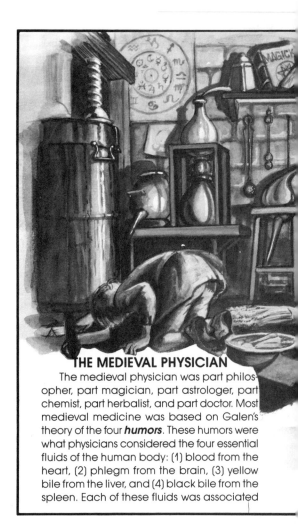

THE MEDIEVAL PHYSICIAN
The medieval physician was part philosopher, part magician, part astrologer, part chemist, part herbalist, and part doctor. Most medieval medicine was based on Galen's theory of the four **humors**. These humors were what physicians considered the four essential fluids of the human body: (1) blood from the heart, (2) phlegm from the brain, (3) yellow bile from the liver, and (4) black bile from the spleen. Each of these fluids was associated

poison was flowing from the heart to the boils."

When the French physician Gentile of Foligno lanced a bubo, he usually dressed it with a plaster made from gum resin, the roots of white lilies, and dried human excrement. Like many medieval physicians, Gentile combined his knowledge of medicine with magic, witchcraft, and **alchemy**, or medieval chemistry. To ward off the plague, he recommended a magic charm made of an amethyst stone set in a gold ring. On the amethyst was carved the figure of

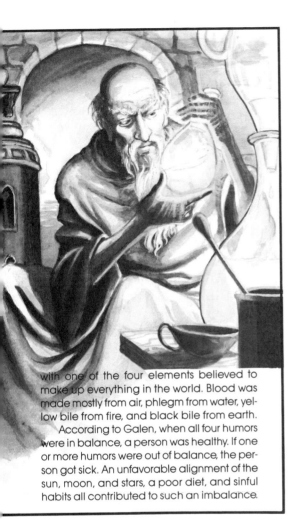

with one of the four elements believed to make up everything in the world. Blood was made mostly from air, phlegm from water, yellow bile from fire, and black bile from earth.

According to Galen, when all four humors were in balance, a person was healthy. If one or more humors were out of balance, the person got sick. An unfavorable alignment of the sun, moon, and stars, a poor diet, and sinful habits all contributed to such an imbalance.

the patient.

If gold was not available, Gentile recommended powdered emerald as the best substitute. Fortunately, the high price of gold and emeralds kept many people from poisoning themselves with Gentile's medicines.

Despite all their remedies and treatments, there is no evidence that the medieval physicians saved a single person from plague. Honest physicians simply admitted that they had no cure. Among them was Gui de Chauliac, one of Paris's most distinguished physicians. De Chauliac expressed his futility this way:

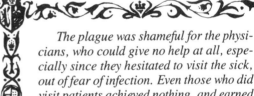

The plague was shameful for the physicians, who could give no help at all, especially since they hesitated to visit the sick, out of fear of infection. Even those who did visit patients achieved nothing, and earned no fees, for all those who caught the plague died, except for a few towards the end of the epidemic who escaped after the buboes had ripened.

a man bowing, with a serpent wrapped around his stomach.

Gentile also treated the plague with internal medicines. Applying his knowledge of alchemy, he believed that an ounce of powdered gold was the most important ingredient in his recipe. The recipe also called for eleven ounces of mercury dissolved by slow heat. After allowing the extremely poisonous mercury to "escape" through heating, the gold was mixed with four cups of water. This mixture was kept airtight over a fire for three days before being served to

Usually, the plague raged on in most cities and villages for two or three months. Then, mysteriously, it would disappear. In this manner, it swept across all of Europe, from Italy in the south to Norway in the north.

By 1350, it had run its course, after sending 25 million people to their graves. Most of the graves were unmarked, but the Black Death left its own mark on every city, village, and family in Europe. It is not a coincidence that most historians say the Middle Ages ended in 1350.

In the first years after the plague, people were filled with shock. Almost every survivor had lost two or three loved ones. It took years to overcome the grief. Even as people returned to their farms or jobs, they could not shake their depression. The plague had altered their outlook and had left them with a constant fear: Would the disease return?

They had to wait only one decade for an answer. In 1362, it did return, and for three years so did the agonizing deaths, the stench of dying bodies, and the mass burials.

This time, the plague claimed another ten million lives, or about one-fourth of the remaining population of Europe. Although the death toll was somewhat lower than it had been during the first plague, the psychological damage may have been even worse. It confirmed the fear that the plague might return at any time.

For three centuries, plague epidemics did return. Most cities experienced a recurrence every ten or fifteen years. Gradually, the epidemics became less widespread, affecting smaller regions instead of the entire continent. Still, no one found a way to cure it or treat it. And for those who caught it, the plague remained as deadly as ever. For nearly three hundred years, it helped keep the population of Europe below thirty million, roughly half what it was before the Black Death.

Eventually, the population of Europe recovered, but the medieval way of life did not. The two most powerful institutions in the Middle Ages were the church and the nobility. After the Black Death, neither one regained the power it had once held.

Many people began to question the church's power. If the plague really was God's punishment, why had the church been unable to obtain God's forgiveness?

The church was further weakened by a severe shortage of priests and nuns. Many of the most devoted churchmen and women had died while trying to comfort the sick. Their replacements were often less dedicated and almost always poorly trained. Gradually, the authority of the church began to erode.

The Black Death also weakened the feudal system. This system depended on the loyalty of vassals and the obedience of peasants to their lords. Before the Black Death, the nobility could usually count on both. After all, land was in

Deaths by Black Death

Deaths in World War II

Deaths in World War I

Americans Killed in War

THE WORST NATURAL DISASTER IN EUROPEAN HISTORY

The Black Death killed about 25 million people at a time when the total population of Europe numbered only about 60 million. It took more lives than both World War I and World War II combined.

such great demand that few noblemen would risk losing their fiefs by breaking a fealty oath. And so many peasants needed food and shelter that they had no choice but to obey their lords. If a rebellious peasant ran away from the village, the lord showed little concern. There were plenty of other peasants to take his or her place.

After the Black Death, the world of the nobility was turned upside down. They still had plenty of land, but suddenly they had a difficult time finding enough peasants to work on it. Peasants were in such demand that they no longer had to work for nothing. Many of them were able to obtain their freedom and demand wages for their work. If a lord refused their demands, they went wherever they could find a better deal.

Members of the nobility did not give up their authority willingly. In England, for example, they used their political power to establish "peasant reform" laws. These laws limited peasants' wages and restricted their freedom. The peasants reacted angrily. With pitchforks, axes, and other crude weapons, they rebelled against the nobility. Historians call this the Peasant Revolt of 1381.

The peasants could not match the military strength of the nobility, but killing peasants or driving them off only added to the nobility's problems. They needed the peasants to work their land. Eventually, they realized that they had to pay them wages and grant them their freedom.

Short of money and labor, many noblemen became more interested in getting money for their land than promises of loyalty or obedience. Instead

of exchanging land for fealty oaths, they sold it or rented it for cash.

Peasants, instead of being bound to the manor, received wages for their work. The most prosperous peasants rented land directly from their former lords and sold their crops for profit. Over the years, some of them even saved enough money to buy their own land.

These changes permanently altered life in the medieval village. The village was no longer the core of medieval society. And the word of the manor lord was no longer law.

With no bondage or sense of loyalty to hold them, many peasants moved out of the villages where their families had lived and worked for centuries. What happened in the village of Millbrook in southern England is a good example.

Records show that after the Black Death, Millbrook was inherited by a landlord who lived hundreds of miles away. When his representatives went to Millbrook to collect taxes in 1360, they found no one living there. In England alone, between the years 1350 and 1400, more than 1,300 villages disappeared.

Instead of living in a multitude of little villages, people began to settle in larger towns. In towns and cities across Europe, the Black Death had created a severe shortage of skilled craftsmen. This led to shortages of tools, clothes, saddles, furniture, and other manufactured goods. Demand for these goods drove the prices so high that many master craftsmen became quite wealthy. Gradually, in order to satisfy the demand for manufactured goods, guilds opened their doors to new city residents. As a result, more and more people began to earn decent wages.

Because the European population was much smaller than it had been before the plague, there were more resources available for everyone. The cities were less crowded, and most citizens were more prosperous. They also became more concerned about their surroundings.

Most cities established public health boards to supervise efficient and sanitary waste disposal. These boards hired "rakers" to remove waste from the city streets. Even these crude sanitation measures made cities more pleasant places to live. More importantly, they helped control the spread of plague and other diseases.

Although most people did not realize it at the time, the Black Death had

not only marked the end of one age but also the beginning of a new one. Today, historians call this new age the **Renaissance**.

During the Renaissance, a more scientific view of the world gradually replaced traditional myths and superstitions. The medical theories of the Middle Ages, which had failed so miserably against the plague, were reexamined. Medical students were expected to have a more accurate understanding of the human body. Dissection and the study of internal organs, both discouraged by the church before the Black Death, became essential to the study of medicine.

The demand for physical proof extended to all fields of learning. Scholars looked less at God's Great Plan and more at His Great Work: the physical universe. Evidence of this shift can be seen in the realism of Renaissance art and in the beginnings of modern chemistry, geology, astronomy, and optics. Galileo built the telescope during the Renaissance, and Copernicus proposed the theory of the solar system. Vasco da Gama charted the west coast of Africa, and Columbus found a "new world."

The Black Death had helped to usher in this new age of exploration. In their pursuit of knowledge, Renaissance scholars laid the foundation for modern science. One thing they were unable to do, however, was find a way to prevent or cure the plague.

Six
Understanding Disease

The last serious outbreak of plague in Europe was the Great Plague of London in 1665. After that, it slowly disappeared from the continent. Elsewhere in the world, plague epidemics have broken out, but none have rivaled the Black Death of 1347-1350.

The cause of the plague remained a mystery until 1894, when an epidemic struck Hong Kong. There a Swiss scientist named Alexandre Yersin discovered the cause of this killer. Thanks to the work of Yersin and other scientists, we now know that the Black Death was a widespread outbreak of an infectious disease called **bubonic plague**. The disease gets its name from the buboes, or swellings, which are its most distinct symptom.

All infectious diseases, including the flu, common cold, measles, chicken pox, tuberculosis, and bubonic plague, are caused by germs, or **microbes** that invade the human body. The microbes that cause bubonic plague are a type of bacteria known as **Yersinia pestis**, or Y. pestis for short. When the Y. pestis bacteria enter the human bloodstream, they concentrate in the **lymph nodes**, just beneath the skin. Here they multiply rapidly, causing the glands to swell and form buboes.

Epidemics of bubonic plague, however, do not start with people. They begin with rats. In fact, bubonic plague normally infects only rats, and rats cannot spread the disease directly to humans. Spreading the disease to humans requires fleas.

The species of flea called the rat flea lives on rats and gets its food by biting rats and sucking their blood. If a flea bites a rat with bubonic plague, it will take in a heavy concentration of Y. pestis bacteria. Then if the flea bites a human, it can inject enough Y. pestis into the person's bloodstream to cause bubonic plague.

Fleas cannot, however, pass the bacteria directly from one human to another. The concentration of Y. pestis in the human bloodstream never gets strong enough for that. Therefore, a flea must first get the bacteria from a rat.

An epidemic of bubonic plague cannot start without large populations of rats and rat fleas. In the Middle Ages, both were abundant. The garbage and human waste in most city streets provided food for millions of rats. There were probably ten times more rats than people in most cities. The rats made their way into the poorly built houses and stables.

Alexandre Yersin

case, why did the disease not appear in Europe before 1347?

Until then, none of the rats in Europe had been infected. Apparently, the first infected rats came to Europe from the Middle East in 1347. They came on ships such as those carrying Genoese merchants to Messina. Rats were so common in those days that no one paid any attention to them.

When officials in Messina saw so many victims of plague on the Genoese merchant ships, they refused to let any people off the ships. But they could not stop the rats. Soon, fleas were spreading bubonic plague from these foreign rats to the native rats. Since most rats lived in or near people's houses, it was not long before fleas were spreading the disease to the people of Messina.

Since a single rat can host hundreds of rat fleas, medieval cities and villages became ideal breeding grounds for bubonic plague. But if this was the

RATS, FLEAS, AND BUBONIC PLAGUE

An outbreak of bubonic plague among humans cannot occur unless three things are present: (1) The *Y. pestis* bacteria that cause the disease, (2) rats, and (3) fleas.

When a flea gets *Y. pestis* bacteria from a rat, the bacteria multiply so fast inside the flea that they completely fill its stomach.

Its stomach becomes so full of bacteria that it cannot digest any blood. This makes the flea so hungry that it will bite anything, including a human. Then it tries to suck blood, even though its stomach is already full. This forces the flea to regurgitate, sending *Y. pestis* bacteria into its victim's bloodstream.

One reason **bubonic plague** finally stopped spreading in Europe was a drastic decline in the rat population. Millions of rats had been killed by bubonic plague. Also, improvements in building construction and sanitation helped keep rats out of people's homes.

This rat flea is magnified 400 times to show it biting into human flesh.

HOW INFECTIOUS DISEASES SPREAD

Only two kinds of **microbes**, or germs, cause **infectious diseases**. These are tiny, single-celled organisms called **bacteria** and even tinier, single-celled organisms called **viruses**. Bacteria and viruses live best in a warm, moist environment.

Some bacteria and viruses are more poisonous than others. Some of them are also more sensitive and die as soon as they are exposed to heat, cold, or dry air. Because of these differences, they have different ways of getting into the bloodstream and causing disease.

Some germs are hardy enough and toxic enough to be transferred through the air. Therefore, people can get some diseases, such as the common cold, by inhaling germs in the air.

Other germs do not infect people unless they touch them directly. People can get these diseases if they handle an object or eat from a utensil that was touched by an infected person.

Germs can also enter the body through open sores on the skin. This is a particularly effective way to transmit germs because the germs enter directly into the bloodstream.

Similarly, some germs, such as the HIV virus that causes AIDS, can only survive in a moist environment. Therefore, they are only passed from one person to another through a direct transfer of blood or other body fluids.

Finally, insects that bite spread diseases very effectively by drawing germs from the blood of one person or animal and depositing them in the blood of another.

Merchants and travelers leaving Messina unknowingly carried infected fleas in their hair, their clothing, and their bundles of merchandise. Wherever they went, they carried fleas. And wherever they stopped, the fleas spread bubonic plague, first to the local rats, and then to the people. This explains why the Black Death followed the major trade routes from one corner of Europe to the other. As merchants, pilgrims, and flagellants followed these routes, they brought the plague with them.

It also explains why no one was able to stop the disease from spreading. While guards at city gates questioned travelers and inspected their cargo, thousands of tiny fleas went unnoticed. Once the plague began to spread through a city, it raged uncontrollably until most of the city's rats had died. Then bubonic plague could not spread.

But from historical records, we know that a plague-like disease did continue to spread. This disease left no ugly buboes or unsightly blisters on the skin, but it did cause an extremely high fever. Then the victim would begin to cough up blood, and in a few days, he or she would die.

Recovery from this disease was almost unheard of. Worst of all, it was more contagious than bubonic plague. If one person began to cough up blood, it was not long before his or her entire household was doomed. No wonder some medieval physicians believed that "looks could kill." The bubonic plague was bad enough, but with the second disease, the death toll soared.

This disease was another form, or strain, of plague called **pneumonic plague**. It is caused by the same bacteria, *Y. pestis*, that cause bubonic plague. This strain is more deadly than bubonic plague because it attacks the lungs.

Although it is more deadly, it can never occur before an outbreak of bubonic plague has occurred. An outbreak of the pneumonic strain begins when bubonic plague attacks a victim who has pneumonia. Then the *Y. pestis* bacteria enter the victim's weakened lungs. Inside the lungs, these bacteria become attached to droplets of water. Within the water droplets, they can be spread into the air whenever the victim breathes, coughs, or chokes. Anyone who inhales these water droplets is likely to catch pneumonic plague.

We have seen how rats from the Middle East brought the bubonic plague to Europe and how it was spread by fleas. However, many historians believe that another important factor also con-

tributed to the Black Death. That factor was population growth.

Throughout the Middle Ages, medieval farming methods and the manorial system of organizing labor had provided most people with food and shelter. By 1347, however, the population had grown too large for this system.

The wealthy nobility held most of the land, and they were unwilling to divide the resources so that everyone had adequate food and shelter. Society could not feed, clothe, and shelter all of its members. This large population was an easy target for plague. The easiest targets of all were the hungry. Their bodies were in no condition to fight off such a contagious disease.

One of the first people to recognize the connection between disease and population growth was an English scientist named Thomas Malthus. In his famous essay, "On the Problem of Population," written in 1877, Malthus said:

The power of population is indefinitely greater than the power of the earth to provide all of man's needs.

In other words, the human population has the potential to grow so large that there will not be enough resources to feed, clothe, and shelter everyone. Malthus maintained that this is what led to the Black Death. The plague was nature's way of balancing the population with the resources available.

Bubonic plague helped control the population of Europe for nearly three centuries. During that time, a smaller, more prosperous population made steady advances in technology. Gradually, these advances made it possible to support a larger population than ever before.

Today, a few cases of bubonic and pneumonic plague still occur in some places in the world every year. But thanks to modern medical technology, another outbreak like the Black Death will never occur. For one thing, we can cure the disease by treating victims with

This special blood cell, magnified more than 4,600 times, is shown capturing harmful bacteria before consuming it.

HOW THE BODY FIGHTS DISEASE

Inside the body, germs multiply rapidly and produce poisonous chemicals, called **toxins**. If the toxins continue to spread unchecked, they can kill you.

Fortunately, the body's **immune system** attacks the toxins. That is what enables you to recover from a disease. This system is made up of billions of white blood cells in the bloodstream. Every one of these white blood cells has a single purpose: to identify and destroy anything that is not part of the human body.

Not all white blood cells are the same, but together they create an amazingly effective communication and defense network. Some are all-purpose "housekeepers." They search and destroy debris in the bloodstream. Others, which scientists call "T cells," attack and kill particular **microbes**. Some of the T cells are memory cells. They circulate in the blood for years and immediately recognize toxins like the ones they destroyed earlier. Still others produce chemical weapons, called **antibodies**, to poison and kill toxins.

Occasionally, enough toxins penetrate this defense system to cause a disease. But every day, the immune system is fighting and winning hundreds of battles with foreign matter that enters our bloodstream.

the **antibiotic** streptomycin. And if several cases of bubonic plague did break out in one city or region today, public health officials would quickly exterminate both rats and fleas in the area.

Since the days of the Black Death, we have come a long way in our ability to fight infectious diseases. Antibiotics are used to combat hundreds of diseases. Others, like polio, German measles, tuberculosis, tetanus, and diptheria, can be prevented with **vaccines**.

Still, we are a long way from conquering disease. In hospital and university laboratories around the world, researchers today are trying to find cures and treatments for leukemia, sickle cell anemia, multiple sclerosis, AIDS, and heart and lung diseases.

It seems that we no sooner find a cure for one disease than another comes along to take its place. Most disturbing, perhaps, are the millions of deaths each year in India, Sudan, Ethiopia, and many African nations caused by diseases of malnutrition. Like the peasants in the Middle Ages, the poor and hungry people in underdeveloped nations today are easy targets for disease.

PREVENTING AND CURING INFECTIOUS DISEASES

Today, **vaccines** and **antibiotics** protect us from many infectious diseases. A vaccine is a weakened form of a disease-carrying **virus**. When you receive an injection of this weakened virus, your white blood cells attack it.

They also develop an immunity to the virus. Some of the white blood cells keep a memory of the virus. The next time it enters your bloodstream, the cells will recognize it and attack it before it can cause serious illness.

Bubonic plague and many other infectious diseases caused by **bacteria** cannot be prevented by vaccine. The next best thing is to cure victims of these diseases by treating them with antibiotics. Antibiotics are drugs that work just like the **antibodies** produced by your own white blood cells. For example, with the aid of the antibiotic streptomycin, your body's **immune system** fights off bubonic or **pneumonic plague** before they have a chance to kill you.

These diseases seem to confirm the theory of Thomas Malthus. At the very least, they pose a serious challenge to modern civilization. Unlike the people of the Middle Ages, we have the resources to feed the hungry. In fact, enormous surpluses of food are harvested in many parts of the world. And we have just begun to tap the food resources available on our lands and in our rivers and seas.

Nevertheless, millions of people around the world continue to starve because the food is not getting into their hands. And as the population continues to grow, it will become more and more difficult to supply food to everyone. For this reason, most experts agree that the greatest challenge facing us today is controlling world population growth. Until we do that, there is little hope of controlling disease.

Glossary

abbey .... A place where a group of monks or nuns live and work.

abbot .... A man who is head of an abbey of monks.

alchemy .... [**AL**-kem-ee] An early form of chemistry often mixed with magic and philosophy.

antibiotic .... [an-ti-by-**OT**-ik] A chemical substance produced by bacteria or fungi that can kill or stop the growth of germs.

antibody .... [**AN**-tee-bod-ee] A protein produced by the body to fight off harmful bacteria.

apprentice .... [uh-**PREN**-tis] A person learning a trade by helping a worker skilled in that trade.

archbishop .... A bishop of the highest rank.

bacteria .... [bak-**TEER**-ee-uh] One-celled organisms that may cause disease.

bailiff .... A person who manages a lord's farms.

bier .... [**BEER**] A stand on which a coffin or dead body is placed before or during a funeral.

bishop .... A priest of high rank in charge of a diocese.

bloodletting .... In medicine, cutting a vein and letting it bleed.

bubo .... [**BYOO**-bo] An inflamed swelling of a lymph node, usually in the armpit or groin.

bubonic plague .... [byoo-**BON**-ik playg] A contagious disease that causes large, painful buboes.

buttress .... A support built against a wall to reinforce it.

chronicler .... [**KRON**-ik-ler] A person who keeps a record of events.

civic court .... The medieval court for petty crimes.

courtier .... [**KOR**-tee-er] An attendant at a royal court.

crossbow .... A mechanical bow with a trigger set on a grooved wooden stock.

diocese .... [**DYE**-uh-sis] The church district under the control of a bishop.

ecclesiastical justice . .[ee-klee-zee-**AS**-ti-kul **JUS**-tis] Medieval system of laws administered by the church.

epidemic . . . .[ep-uh-**DEM**-ik] The rapid spreading of a disease to many people.

extreme unction . . . . . .In the Catholic Church, the final blessing given to a dying person.

fealty oath . . . .[**FEEL**-tee oath] A loyalty oath between two lords, one of whom is more powerful than the other.

feudalism . . . .[**FEW**-dul-ism] The political organization in which land is held by vassals in return for their loyalty and service to more powerful lords.

fief . . . .[**FEEF**] A piece of land held by a vassal.

flagellant . . . .[**FLA**-jell-unt] A person who takes part in flagellation, or self-beatings, as a religious discipline.

flagellation . . . .[fla-jell-**A**-shun] The practice of self-beating for religious discipline.

freeman . . . . .A person, usually a skilled craftsman, who lives and works in a village, and receives payment for his labor.

guild . . . .[**GILD**] An association of merchants or skilled craftsmen.

halberd . . . . .A medieval weapon that is like a spear and battle-ax combined.

heresy . . . .[**HARE**-is-ee] A religious belief condemned by the church.

hierarchy . . . .[**HIRE**-ark-key] A system in which there are higher and lower positions of power, such as the noble ranks of king, duke, earl, etc.

high justice . . . . .Justice administered by the nobility for serious crimes.

humors . . . . .The four body fluids believed by medieval physicians to be responsible for one's health.

immune system . . . . . .[im-**MEWN SIS**-tem] The body's system of protecting itself from disease or infection.

infectious disease . . . .[in-**FEK**-shuss dis-**EASE**] A disease that tends to spread to others.

inheritance . . . . [in-**HARE**-i-tunce] That which is handed down from one generation to the next, such as land, money, or keepsakes.

jousting tournament . . A contest in which knights on horseback use lances to knock each other off their horses.

keep . . . . The main building in a castle.

lance . . . . A weapon made of a long pole with a pointed metal tip.

lord . . . . A person who rules an estate.

lymph node . . . . [**LIMF** node] A small mass of tissue that is part of the lymphatic system located just beneath the skin. Lymph nodes produce white blood cells.

mace . . . . A heavy club with a metal head, usually with spikes.

manor . . . . Land belonging to a noble lord that is partly divided among peasants.

manorialism . . . . [man-**OR**-ee-ul-ism] The social system under which peasants are bound to serve the lord of a manor.

master . . . . An expert in a craft or trade.

Maundy Thursday . . . . [**MAWN**-dee **THURS**-day] The Thursday before Easter, also called "Holy Thursday."

medieval . . . . [mid-**EE**-vul] Pertaining to the Middle Ages.

microbe . . . . [**MIKE**-robe] Any living thing, such as a disease germ, that is too tiny to be seen without a microscope.

Middle Ages . . . . The period in European history between ancient and modern times, approximately A.D. 800-1350.

monastery . . . . [**MON**-us-stare-ee] A place where monks live.

monk . . . . [**MUNK**] A man who belongs to a religious order whose members live in a monastery.

nobility . . . . The small minority of wealthy landowners with special titles or rank assigned by royalty.

pestilence . . . . [**PEST**-ill-unce] A deadly disease that spreads rapidly from person to person.

pillory . . . . [**PILL**-or-ee] A wooden board with holes in which the head and hands can be locked.

pneumonic plague . . . . [new-**MON**-ik playg] A disease of the lungs caused by the same bacteria as bubonic plague.

pope . . . . The bishop who is head of the Roman Catholic Church.

quarantine . . . . [**KWOR**-un-teen] To keep a diseased person, animal, or plant away from others so that the disease will not spread.

reeve . . . . A trusted peasant who serves as foreman of a manor.

Renaissance . . . . [**REN**-uh-sonce] The great revival of art and learning in Europe between 1400 and 1600.

scourge . . . . [**SKURJ**] A small whip.

serf . . . . A person legally bound to serve a manor for life.

sexton . . . . A person who performs minor church duties such as ringing bells and digging graves.

siege . . . . [**SEEJ**] The surrounding of a city, fort, or castle, by an enemy army trying to capture it.

squire . . . . A young man training to become a knight.

steward . . . . A person who manages daily affairs of the manor.

Tatars . . . . [**TOT**-urs] Mongolian warriors who invaded western Asia in the Middle Ages.

tithe . . . . A portion of one's earnings, traditionally one tenth, paid to the church.

town crier . . . . A person who shouts public announcements through the streets of a village or town.

toxin . . . . A poison produced by the bacteria or viruses that cause disease.

vaccine . . . . [vak-**SEEN**] Any substance made up of killed or weakened bacteria or virus that is put into the body to create antibodies and prevent disease.

vassal . . . . [**VASS**-ul] A nobleman in the feudal system who holds land in return for a promise of loyalty and helping a more powerful lord in war.

virus . . . . A form of matter, smaller than any bacteria, that can multiply in living cells and cause disease.

Yersinia pestis . . . . [yer-**SIN**-ee-uh **PEST**-us] The bacteria that cause bubonic plague.

Further Reading

MIDDLE AGES

Brooks, Polly Schoyer. *World of Walls: The Middle Ages in Western Europe*. Philadelphia: Lippincott, 1966.

Brown, Reginald Allen. *Castles*. London: Batsford, 1954.

Buehr, Walter. *Knights and Castles and Feudal Life*. New York: Putnam, 1957.

Clifford, Alan. *The Middle Ages*. St. Paul, Minnesota: Greenhaven Press, 1980.

Cootes, Ronald J. *The Middle Ages*. White Plains, New York: Longman, 1980.

Pierre, Miguel. *The Days of Knights and Castles*. Translated by Penny Davies. Morristown, New Jersey: Silver Burdett, 1980.

Reeves, Marjorie. *The Medieval Town*. White Plains, New York: Longman, 1954.

Reeves, Marjorie. *The Medieval Village*. White Plains, New York: Longman, 1954.

Sobel, Donald J. *The First Book of Medieval Man*. New York: Franklin Watts, 1959.

Terry, Arthur Guy. *Lord and Vassal*. New York: Row, Peterson, 1926.

Warner, Phillip. *The Medieval Castle*. New York: Taplinger, 1971.

Williams, Jay. *Life in the Middle Ages*. New York: Random House, 1966.

MEDICINE AND DISEASE

Beizer, Melvin. *Germs Make Me Sick!* New York: Crowell, 1985.

LeMaster, Leslie Jean. *Bacteria and Viruses*. Chicago: Children's Press, 1985.

Lewis, Lucia Zylak. *First Book of Microbes*. New York: Franklin Watts, 1955.

Loeble, Suzanne. *Fighting the Unseen*. New York: Abelard Schuman, 1967.

Nourse, Alan Edward. *Viruses*. New York: Franklin Watts, 1983.

Turner, Derek. *The Black Death*. White Plains, New York: Longman, 1978.

Other Works Consulted

Boccaccio, Giovanni. *The Decameron.* Translated by G.H. McWilliam. New York: Penguin Books, 1972.

Bowsky, William M., ed. *The Black Death: A Turning Point in History?* Melbourne, Florida: Krieger, 1978.

Burke, James. *The Day the Universe Changed.* Boston: Little, Brown & Co., 1985.

Cartwright, Frederick F. *Disease and History.* New York: New American Library, 1972.

Coulton, George Gordon. *The Medieval Scene.* Cambridge, England: University Press, 1967.

Deaux, George. *The Black Death.* New York: Weybright and Tolley, 1966.

Delauney, Albert, et al. *The World of Microbes.* Garden City, New York: Doubleday, 1965.

Dubos, Rene. *Health and Disease.* New York: Time, 1965.

Durant, Will. *The Age of Faith.* New York: Simon & Schuster, 1950.

Gardner, John. *The Life and Times of Chaucer.* New York: Knopf, 1977.

Golden, Abner and Powell, Deborah E. *Understanding Human Disease.* Baltimore: Williams & Wilkins, 1985.

Gottfried, Robert S. *The Black Death: Natural and Human Disaster in Medieval Europe.* New York: Free Press, 1983.

Huizinga, Johan. *The Waning of the Middle Ages.* Translated by F. Hopman. London: E. Arnold & Co., 1924.

Kent, Thomas H. and Hart, Michael N. *Introduction to Human Disease.* East Norwalk, Connecticut: Appleton & Lange, 1986.

Koch, H.W. *Medieval Warfare.* New York: Crescent Books, 1978.

Larkin, P.J. *Medieval World.* Chester Springs, Pennsylvania: Dufour, 1980.

Malthus, Thomas Robert. *Essay on Population.* New York: Dutton, 1878, reprinted 1958.

McNeill, William H. *Plagues and People.* Garden City, New York: Doubleday, 1976.

Nohl, Johannes. *The Black Death: A Chronicle of the Plague.* Translated by C.H. Clarke. New York: Harper & Row, 1969.

Rowling, Marjorie. *Life in Medieval Times.* New York: Putnam, 1968.

Zacour, Norman. *An Introduction to Medieval Institutions.* New York: St. Martin's Press, 1969.

Zeigler, Phillip. *The Black Death.* New York: Harper & Row, 1969.

Zinsser, Hans. *Rats, Mice and History.* New York: Bantam, 1965.

Index

The Author, Timothy Levi Biel was born and raised in eastern Montana. A graduate of Rocky Mountain College, he received a Ph.D. in literary studies from Washington State University.

He is the author of numerous nonfiction books, many of which are part of the hightly acclaimed Zoobooks series for young readers. In addition, he has written *Pompeii: World Disasters* and is the editor of the World Disaster Series.

Illustrations by Maurie Manning and Michael Spackman capture the drama of the events described in this book. Manning majored in illustration at Massachusetts College of Art in Boston and has been a professional children's illustrator for more than six years. Her work appears regularly in such magazines as *Children's Digest, Humpty Dumpty,* and *Highlights for Children.*

A designer and professional illustrator for more than nineteen years, Spackman has experience as both a portraitist and commercial illustrator. He received his training at the High Museum Academy of Art in Atlanta.